FALLING APPLES

Matt Mooney

ORIGINAL WRITING

© 2010 Matt Mooney

Cover design by Garreth Joyce & Siobhán Mooney

The Irish poems have been previously published in the magazine *Feasta*

ISBN: 978-1-907179-56-3

A CIP catalogue for this book is available from the National Library.

Published by ORIGINAL WRITING LTD., Dublin, 2010.

Printed in Great Britain by the MPG Books Group, Bodmin and King's Lynn

FOREWORD

The poems in *Falling Apples* have a deceptively light and approachable flair. These are poems that come naturally to the ear and offer an imaginative and direct solace of words in the clutter of our contemporary world's roar and blast. Taken together they constitute a 'conversation without speaking,' as is stated in the poem, *The Romanian*. We are all in transit and experience is merely a handful of images we pick up along the way, fleeting and often forgettable. Matt Mooney has managed to create a small and lucid guidebook for the imagination's heart and head, whether contemplating a scene in winter, whose silence and ordinariness reflect upon our own silent voices, or visiting a foreign place. How is personal experience to be measured, if not by these small and private steps? There is also, in terms of style, a quiet mastery at work here which does not hamper the reader's own powers, in private, of interpretation; Mooney is effectively telling stories, personal narratives, and giving the reader unimposing directions at the same time. In *Snakes Alive* there is a Pandora's Box-like warning implicit in this snapshot, a morality tale, in which what fascinates us and that which we imagine we can tame can turn on us; this is a parable for the hubris of our times. So it cannot be said that Mooney concentrates merely on personal observations or has written up a series of pleasing images. There is an unsettling sense of the poet's divination here, of our lack of mastery of the world through which we wander, restricted, to whatever degree, by our own moral gravity. A meaningful and challenging collection.

Fred Johnston

Introduction

Matt Mooney's second collection of poetry 'Falling Apples' will delight and inspire. On a wide canvas he depicts a panorama of experiences, scenes, nature and events. The collection takes us on a whirlwind journey from his native Galway, to Thailand, to New Zealand, to his home in Listowel and many places in between.

The poems have an immediacy and tenderness in the observation of nature:

> *'Breathless with wonderment'* in 'Badgers in the Wood';

> *'Kookaburras came like Carmelites,*
> *Reverently in twos'* in 'By the Pond'.

His butterfly in 'Soft Trap' leaves him *'weightless in her space.'*

Matt's words are carefully chosen for their colour and sound to evoke just the right note: his cat *'Soft stepping, white bibbed and black'* and *'The fixing of scarves and tumbling outdoors.'* In the pub his friends are *'Using pints for punctuation.'*

Sounds abound as in *'Muffled whoops of cygnet swan delight.'* We have the masterly depiction in the 'The Glass Blower' of the new glass:

> *'Snipped slim like a slender candle*
> *With its pointed lips and its lily look*
> *It stands proud of its wily master.'*

Matt's love of music is reflected in the lyricism of his nature and love poems. The translation of these written in French and Irish give an added dimension to the intensity of feeling. The result is a powerful transmission of the emotion felt.

His meditative philosophical poems are reminiscent of the Metaphysical poets of the past.

The collection is peopled by old friends and family. Good poetry universalises experiences and reminds us of ourselves and our feelings. What parent hasn't experienced the anxiety and relief of a child's late-night homecoming. 'Late Night Taxi' hits the spot!

Some of the poems reflect the complexities and convolutions of life and have a social and political context. There is an empathy with refugees and prisoners in their lost identities and dignity.

The poet bemoans the destruction of the landscape and hills *'acupunctured'* by wind turbines. *'The smooth black shining motorway'* devoid of colour and life is in sharp contrast to:

'Rustling the ditch's floral skirt for strawberries,
Red and wild, elusive little rubies of delight'.

This indeed is a delightful collection. We have a new voice in the Irish poetry scene. Read **Falling Apples** and be delighted and charmed.

Madeleine O' Sullivan.

Contents

FALLING APPLES

I'm up to my eyes in apples,
Lizard like upon the trunk;
Heavy branches to be shaken,
Fishing for the furthest fruit:
Ripened red and yellow faces
High on top beneath the sun.

I'm in a ball filled bouncer
But I'm careful not to fall-
Just now I ducked my head
From flying fruit going down
To hop like heavy hailstones
In a shower upon the ground.

Diversion

Sonny O'Dea, our Master's mate,
Closed the gate and lifted the latch
Of the door painted in national green
After he tied up his jennet outside.

His brown hat had no ribbon band,
It was turned up here and up there.
It sheltered him in the wind and rain
And shaded his face from the sun.

His coat, a corn bag from his barn,
Was fastened with a single horse nail;
His step so slow had a ring of steel
From the tips of his hobnailed boots.

Over the road we could see him come
And Sonny O'Dea didn't have to knock;
It was just our grammatical grilling time-
That blasted blitz for us at two o'clock!

So with one voice we sang in chorus
'Tá fear sa halla' ('A man in the hall');
We knew we were in for some fun
As the Master would answer the call.

Sonny spoke out like an Indian chief,
The Master's voice was always even-
Whatever was said we hadn't a care
Once they had a long conversation;
That would help at the end of the day
To shorten a little our long education.

This is your Captain speaking

'This is your Captain speaking'
The voice ground out with gravity.
I suddenly sat up straight in my seat
To hear what was the calamity!
Yes, we had ascended successfully,
Levelled off and headed for London-
But somehow we were lacking in thrust
So my feelings were somewhat deflated.
'We have been told by Shannon control
That a hatch has been left open'-
'Oh Lord our God' I said 'What?'
And he added 'There's no safety risk
At all and we are returning to Shannon.'
As he turned around there wasn't a sound
Nor a sight of our pretty hostesses.

I thought of the news on *Five Seven Live*
And cast the bad thought from my mind;
After all of this crisis without any crash
We had our hatch shut up in Shannon.

Beside me sat a young businessman
With a hint of a beard of maturity
Who had been asleep quite oblivious,
But on the second time round
He awoke back on the ground
And I told him of all that had happened.

Needless to say he was taken aback,
Thinking he was landed safely in England;
So we laughed at our lot as airborne we got
While the Captain made up for delaying us!
And all of a sudden the staff reappeared
To serve tea from behind the drawn curtains
And instead of landing in London at five
We were happy we landed at half past, alive!

OVERHEARD

'I should have known

He'd want to get up on the wall.

Hold on to him that's all-

And don't let him fall!'

Carnival

The half moon begins its harvest climb;
This night is sure to be as bright as day.
The turf fires kindle and flame into life
In the hillside homes this evening time.

From across the Racecourse and the river
Carnival sounds drift in the still cool air
And rainbow rows of festive lights in town
Send up a crowning glow that spreads
And floods the gently sloping fields afar.

Lake Te Anau

Stopping at Lake Te Anau
Felt like we had stumbled
On some masterpiece of art
Then made a part of it;
To be of no other tableau-
So perfect and untamed.

Breathless at the stillness
Of lake water pastel blue:
Nature's ancient mirror
For the clearest of a sky
And Keplar snowy crested-
True reflections in Te Anau.

SIESTA

Sliabh Mish in Summer:
Her lows and highs beyond
The fields that lie
Beside Tralee at Boherbee,
Where in the sun
In front of Dunnes
The shoppers
Filter in and out;
While sleepy breezes
Find their way
From Tralee Bay
To fill the afternoon
With sea wine from
The Maharees;
Or to have sweet reveries
Of sharing a siesta
With that mountain,
Guardian of the town,
Beneath its eiderdown
Spun from clouds
In bridal white that lie
On curves and crests
Along a blue horizon
Of a day in time.

SKYLIGHT TO THE STARS

Skylight of pine like a picture frame,
Only eye of my sleepless musing;
What strikes me at this hour of dreams
Is the single star that looks at me
From the depths of our lovely universe.

I'd love to know if the builders charged
For your beacon light so gifted;
As I lie on my back my thoughts of black
Slip away with the blind I've lifted.

Now I think of today by the River Rhone
And hills so high with slopes of trees
Where hosts of village houses stand;
St. Galmier, its square with cafés there;
A fruit shop of reds and yellows;
A church of stone standing all alone,
Its walls being cleansed by craftsmen.

While alas I lie and look on high
And muse on the higher heavens
I have found it wise to think of time
For the dawn has stolen my star away
And all that's left to me today
Is a frame with a bright blue canvas.

Thistledown

Thistledown: flight so light,
Floating summertime on river air;
On the bank first kisses.

ALLURING

A woman's smile can haul her sailor boy ashore;
With just a single kiss she lures him on her line.

OUTSIDE

Afterwards
Under the eiderdown
We lie inert;
Alert to night winds
That hurry up the hill,
Playing 'hide and seek'
Among the trees;
Lulling us to sleep,
Sure of ourselves
And the only sounds
Outside.

SOLITUDE

Aux revoirs à la porte ouverte
Un très beau Dimanche en été;
Dans le ciel un avion brillait;
Chez moi c'est très solitaire.

En ville à l'heure de la messe-
Le secret de la paix à la Place;
Personne ne bougait, ne parlait;
Avec le journal je suis rentré.

Mes chiens m'ont bien reçus;
Au téléphone un appel amical-
Voilà ma fille qui s'est levée!
Encore tout a bien tourné.

Encore une fois je pouvais voir
La beauté de montagnes au loin;
Comme un train d'un tunnel noir,
Je suis rentré dans la lumière.

ALONE

Goodbyes at the open front door
On a Sunday morning in summer.
An aeroplane shines in the sun;
At home I can learn about solitude.

In the town it's midday mass time-
A time and a place to be peaceful,
A short truce in the struggle of life;
I purchase the Sunday Press paper.

I'm welcomed in home by the dogs
And a friendly telephone caller;
My daughter awakes at it's ringing,
Once again my world is revolving.

I am able to admire the day's beauty-
The far distant mountains before me;
Like a train from a tunnel emerging
I have returned to the lap of creation.

Stepping Away

Using pints for punctuation,
Farming friends around him,
Holding earthy conversations:
Man to man discussions
On someone's lock of cattle
Or a lovely score of lambs.

Turning his back to the bar,
Measuring his every step,
He employs a walking stick
To aid his disappearance;
Exiting black swing doors,
Writing off another night.

In good humour going home,
Unconscious of the loneliness
Of the silent sleeping village,
He sits into my waiting car
And we leave the streetlamps
To the phantoms of the night.

Swan Delight

These are the dark days of the winter, short and stormy;
The wind and the driving rain rebuff the flowerless furze.
The sycamore and the beech that were so fair out there
Stand bleakly staring into space, uncertain of their fate.

And I am thinking of the swans in the bog of Ballinagare.
They have never left my mind, come rain or come shine,
Ever since three cygnets grey swooped above my head,
Over the rusty metal bridge that spanned the broad river.

All three flew low and wide around and then they landed
Downstream with muffled whoops of cygnet swan delight;
Heads held in the air, graceful as the Viking ships at sea;
They were close to me where I was the undercover man.

My water skiers with loud whirring of their musical wings
Skimmed along the surface of the river to westwards fly
To their chosen spot where they could swim alone, apart;
At that I felt a touch of loss to think of mine gone far away.

But one evening from the road I saw them all assembled,
All a gaggle in a green bog field beside the flowing river;
Seeing five more fly in to land the rest below paraded,
Their chanting windpipes all in tune in a place deserted.

WHERE HEMISPHERES MEET

Self-contained in self drive cars:
Families, my daughter's and my own,
In a blue Focus and a light blue Fiesta,
Driving always in formation-
Our sights were set on Milford Sound.

We stopped at times by chasms.
Stunned by haloed mountain peaks;
Boundless acres of countless sheep.

Eating at a roadhouse at a cross
Where the chimney with its log fire
Filled us with New Zealand lore.

Now the evening's endless mountains
Throw the cloak of twilight round us.

Daughters in exile in Australia
Travel with us on the road tonight;
So far, so long, now all together,
Hemispheres had found each other.

Oasis

The warm balm of the velvet breeze
Wafts around the bungalow gable
By the sheltering sycamore trees,
Caressing my face at the table.

Soft stepping, white bibbed and black,
The cat settles down in the sun
And on the leaves he lays on his back,
Russet bed by the autumn spun.

The simple song of the robin red,
Plain chant of the solo singer;
Stepladder up to the hedge ahead,
Standing by for a tasty trimmer.

Black and white and quick and low,
Magpies cruise with crackling chatter;
The cars gone by on the road below
Restoring the peace that they shatter.

Soft Trap

A Painted Lady butterfly
Delays delicately nearby,
Her freshness never old.

Wings of words unspoken,
I'm weightless in her space.

Then a ripe red apple falls
With a faint silent sob,
Soft trapping me in sunshine
In the orchard by the stream.

At last I have to walk away
But I leave my pain behind me
Where quietly clamour now
The sniping stinging wasps.

SOUND EFFECTS

In South Kerry from a narrow mountain road
That hung above the farmsteads by the sea
I saw a cattle run and heard the cuckoo call:
A sudden motion towards the surging ocean
And a voice saying it's summer time again.

There were roadworks at Coomakista Pass
Making wide the wayward route to Waterville:
Giant kango hammers cracking roadside rock
At Caherdaniel; machines to move mountains.

In the Golden Cove behind the Sneem Hotel
Six strong oarsmen dipped their oars as one,
Striking the evening silence with an even beat
As slowly a lonesome swan took centre stage,
Cruising at a steady pace on waters of ebony.

HER APOLLO

His characters all came alive,
Stepping on the stage of time:
The playwright and the poet,
Words flowing like good wine.

On the mall of the main street
His statue stands forever,
Cap in hand and in his stride-
A man for walking by the river.

Passing the Apollo of her dreams
His widow softly touched him then,
Knowing that unseen angels
Were taking gentle care of him.

Our Laughing Cavalier

Johnny our postman flew off on his bike
Across the bridge on the river low down;
As alive as a hare just sprung from his lair,
He was primed up for doing his rounds.

As merry a postman as ever I have seen
Who possessed the great gift of the gab,
Though we lived at the end of his daily run
Yet he'd still be as fresh and as full of fun

As when he threw his bag up on his back
At the door of his little thatched cottage,
That was perched on the side of the street-
The main road that ran through the village.

He'd whistle and sing as if he were king
And his heart was so light on his bicycle;
He'd sit up like he owned half of Ireland.
At the time there were men in their fields

Who worked with ponies and horses.
They'd all say "The postman! " then wave
And exchange a few words on the weather;
If he had his way it wouldn't rain ever.

All the news still unread in his satchel,
As he pedalled and freewheeled ahead,
Would not be as bad as anyone thought.
He hoped for them all 't would be good.

Our laughing cavalier, down off his bike,
Would half dance in our path to the door,
Deliver the mail to my mother awaiting
Then maybe he'd waltz 'round the floor.

As he talked he would look at you straight
And you saw that his eyes were so brown,
Filled with laughter and lovable roguery-
He helped you forget the day's drudgery.

RIVER FIELDS

There is something in the setting sun
That speaks to me of death and darkness
As the dying moments of another day
Are suffused with a splash of crimson.
Now the surface of the Feale turns red
By Martin Daly's low lying river fields,
Near the large crucifix at Convent Cross.

THE BALLAD OF BRYAN MCMAHON

It was on the eve of Valentine
In the year of ninety eight
That the Master's name so resonant
Was marked absent on the slate;
So delicate were the daffodils
After days of winter strife
When the soul of Bryan Mac Mahon
Went through the Gap of Life.

So silent now the river Feale,
They had shared the sun together,
For the Master of all masters
Has called Bryan to Him forever;
Our nation maker is close to God
Whose gifts he'll hand us down:
Like words to lips and songs to sing
In his native Kerry town.

Away he'll send on flights of doves
Through heaven's open door
His love by Gort a'Ghleanna
In the vale of Knockanure;
He was the master and the writer
Whose gifts he left behind:
Like pride to last in his native place
And his books to feed the mind.

He loved the Fleadh's homecoming
And the folk who travelled far
To sing and dance in the sunny Square
Or to play in any bar;
He'd always watch the marching bands
As they passed with a great hurrah!
He'd stand at his door in the evening sun
To watch the mardi gras.

Our footpaths miss his noble steps:
He was a father to the town;
His greeting marked you present-
"Conas tán tú? Tán tú ann! "
So when you're walking down the street
Know that we've only got today
And sometimes stop and chat awhile
For that was Bryan's way.

THE GLASS BLOWER

In St.Galmier by the River Rhone,
With its mineral waters of renown,
In an atelier you'll see a souffleur.

The furnace heat is orange bright,
So hot it has to be before he can
With taps and turns on his bench
Mould the sand on a magic wand
To any form in the master's mind.

On the tip of the rod a body round
Builds on its stem to form the base
Of the final glass and its equilibrium.

All circles run round the rod's end;
With his wrist he twists and twirls.
For him it spins into a vase of blue,
Snipped slim like a slender candle:
With its pouting lips and its lily look
It stands up proud of its wily master.

THE SIGNALMAN

I see him as the signalman
On the unseen tracks of time:
A family priest for all of us-
As we travel down the line.

Railway stations made him blue
When young and leaving home-
I wonder if it was his Signalman
That for so long kept him going?

He taught the boys of Wexford
By the Barrow in New Ross
And at a later time the Déise lads
In Dungarvan's lovely town;
A chaplin in Dublin's Liberties,
Now in Limerick nearer home;
The road that led to his priesthood
Had earlier started off in Rome.

In his vestments with a bell of brass
Before the quarter past eleven mass,
Ringing out "Come all ye within"
To that little hospital Chapel
That always has been dear to him.

St. Augustine's "Lord we are restless
Until we rest with Thee"
He quoted freely at his Golden Jubilee.

He has always been our signalman
Along the unseen tracks of time:
A family priest for everyone
As we are travelling down the line.

TOM MOON

Tom Moon as he sat in our kitchen some days
Turned the talk into song and before very long
He'd start pacing the floor from table to door,
Look into the mirror used for Saturday shaving,
Tilt back his hat and in a voice that was deep
Sing loud with a chorus a love song sonorous;
Alas at the end of the story of loving her dearly
They 'parted forever on the banks of the Lee.'

Later on in his life he worked in the forestry
And he lived down at the foot of the mountain;
How happy he was one day when I called to him
And he got his young daughter to dance for us.

While we drank a few bottles of stout
He sang from his heart of this beautiful lady
In the wonderful words of her lover lamenting:
Looking at her picture he'd hung on the wall
He gazed at her face and thought that if only
She was really alive and holding his hand
Like the time they were two lovers together.

Though dead and gone I think of his songs:
I hear his musical voice full of merriment.
Now I often sing too as he himself used to do
For it makes our hearts beat that much better.
Join in yourself and you'll feel the same joy
For Tom Moon in his day was a minstrel boy.

VILLAGE LADY

"Peig my dear, no, I won't have tea; "
To look at you there in your armchair,
Your hair so white in the window light,
Is good enough for me you see;
You say your beads you have said-
For the road ahead.

You're on decade nine of your dream
Near Coolnaleen, where falls a stream
From Sliabh Chathail on high,
Flowing into the Feale that's nearby.

Your Tanavalla forever
Looking down to the river;
In the cot that's your own
By the fireside alone,
Widowed but merry-
"You'll have whiskey or sherry, "
"It's not often you call-
I'll tell no one at all"
"I have had the hedge cut," she said,
"And the turf's in the shed."
"My son Mike will be home
In the fall of the year;
My daughter Noreen is living so near,
We're over and back
Every day of the year; "

"To Jo's I'd go, up the hill long ago,
Past Johnny's I'd climb-
One step at a time;
Up the Dale Road to me
Came my dear friend Mary."
"They were all great, " she said,
"It's a pity they are dead."
"Well I miss Dr. Jack-
When I think and look back:
How he'd call from the town
And come in and sit down."

"Do you know Fr. Pat?
I'll tell you now Matt:
He was here yesterday
And I said when I pray
My prayers in Irish I say;
I learned them when young,
Off by heart one by one."

"In the old school in Clounmacon
There was skipping and jumping,
Ring a rosy and all kinds of fooling;
That time all the neighbours
At the end of their labours
Danced the polka then Patsy Haley,
And rose in the morning so early."

She had an old local song
That was not very long,
It was all about poor old Michael J,
'To O'Connor's Grove
They used to rove,
All Tullamore did say.'
I could go on but Peig is gone,
With memories so sweet-
She might you know have the rest of that
When again, I hope, we'll meet.

Red Orange Juice

The cypress trees that line the road are tall and trim
Like sentinels of the forests and the fields
That clothe the Tuscan hills in green and gold.
Past the castle of Gargonza near Monte San Savino
And many hairpin bends that tease you as you travel,
You reach the gates of Siena-a city lost in time.

It's Gothic Square is strangely shell shaped,
Houses standing seven stories high above you;
Shutters drawn for coolness in the afternoon-
Faded, old and medieval, like a massive backdrop.

Weary now, we had climbed up earlier to the city
Sometimes out of breath—not just from the beauty
That lay ahead or round about and down below;
The sun suggesting a long cool drink above.

On the cobblestones the students squat; children play,
Chasing the pigeons that fly low among them;
Red orange juice on the shaded restaurant table.

Bilbao Interlude

By the banks of the Nervión river
In the cool of the chestnut trees
I watched a wayward fallen leaf
Tumbling along in the breeze;
Touching my bare sandaled toes
It said 'Time passes quickly by'
And I thought as it floated away
That it went with a hint of a sigh.

Trams green and black in Bilbao
That sound as low as our prayers;
Then a city centre bus sped by
And it made me sit up and stare
At a dressed up matron seated
With knitting needles and wool.
Or so I was fooled into thinking-
By an image so very well done.

Cois Laoi

Fear ard a chromann síos,
A leag a shúil ar ní thíos faoi:
Cúig cent ar lána an bhus,
A bhogann thart gan mhoill
Le teacht tráthnóna fhuadraigh
I gcathair chroíúil Chorcaí.

Micléinn ag filleadh abhaile
Chun ocras an lae a mharú
Thuas i seomraí 'tá acu ar cíos
Thall i dTobar Rí an Domhnaigh.

Cois abhann do shiúlamar:
Scathán de chrainn is binsí
Ag bun gháirdíní na n-uasal-
A gcuid staighrí sios le fána;
Lanúin óg ag blaiseadh póg,
Na lachain ag snámh le chéile.

San óstán tá siamsa is sólás,
Ceol faoi choinnleoir craobhach,
Seaimpéin is gloiní seanga:
Corc ag popáil, gáire is gean,
An oíche sa chathair ag titim.

ALIVE BY THE LEE

A tall man bends low,
While there is time,
To pick up a lost coin
Lying in the bus lane,
Before the evening rush.

Students heading home
Hungry for their dinner
High up in rented rooms
Across the Shaky Bridge
Up there in Sunday's Well.

We walked by the Lee,
A looking glass for trees;
First kisses on a bench
As wild ducks pair away.

Sunset on the Western Rd.
Now an avenue of gold;
Blackbirds begin to sing
Around the Pink Clinic-
Place of human healing.

On a building site next door
A dumper driver on overtime,
Working till the last light of day,
Dumps another load of rubble
On a heap of stone and clay.

In the new hotel, the Kingsley,
Champagne in slender glasses;
Popping corks, loud laughter
And the night falling in the city;
The sweet music of a harp
Scintillating under chandeliers.

St. Malo Maid

Spin and pirouette petite fille
Spin and pivot chère Charlotte,
Spin round and round my head.
Spin when your coat is shed,
Spin the draw drum of my dreams.
Spin you dancing poppy doll,
Spin you airborne spinning top-
Spin me as well St. Malo maid.
Spin and kick above your head-
Spin until you reach the galaxy,
Spin with stardust in your hands.
Spin female phantom of the night,
Spin slow away and say goodbye;
Spin soon again, I'll see you then,
Spin back to me and to me smile.

TUNES

To the bodhrán's beat your heart's in harmony,
Sinews plainly dance in the player's timing foot;
From head to toes our traditional music flows-
Like it does on piano strings it vibrates below.

The sitting down around, the resining of the bow;
The tuning up is done and a fiddler plays a tune-
The spirit of the session comes suddenly to life.
Now listen to the rhythm of the music of the night.

Waltzing at the Fleadh

In Clonmel the earnest Fleadh lovers
Walk around the streets of the town
In search of the best of the sessions
While the river Suir flows quietly on.

The couples wheel round in full circle
In sets danced by the young and old:
Sidestep, swing and cross over again,
Round the house, now dance in a ring.

We Tennessee waltzed by Heron's
To the strains of a sweet violin
Held in the hands of that talented man-
Jim McKillop from Antrim himself.

On Monday the sidewalk was sunny
By the walls of the Arm's Hotel
And the royalty of traditional music
Were there from the county of Meath.

For us the newly crowned champions
Began playing to begin their new day;
Troy Bannon was the céilí band leader
On the concert flute showing the way.

CARPENTER'S SON

High up over nearby Bantry Bay
Nails are hammered into wood
On the town library roof above us:
Maybe staccato accompaniment
To enliven poetry reading tones.

As every nail went home to stay
Like words and lines and stops
I couldn't but imagine it was Him
From Nazareth-a carpenter's son.

Son of the carpenter fix me too
And make my heart your home:
Tap tap the nails we never feel-
Your damaged goods in transit;
Tap, tap tap and hammer home,
Let hand and eye align each line,
Then finish off what was begun
The day you created me in time.

Make and shape me as you wish,
Perfect, direct and aim me straight.
Feed me with your spiritual food
To take me to your home away
And when it is your chosen day
Let me be in a sinless state;
Shape me sing me write me down-
Great poet and carpenter's son.

Eyes of the Glen

One night we slept in Glendalough
Above the Abhainn Mhór river,
Its mountain waters wild and brown
From Parnell's place in Avondale
To Moore's Avoca winding ever.

The little fields climbed up the glen
Embroidered with sheep and lambs;
Deep down below a constant flow
That sounds around the river rocks.

Stepping stones to a trodden path
In the shade of the Wicklow woods
To walk to Saint Kevin's holy lakes,
Each a glimmer in the eyes of God.

Calm lakes to quench a thirsty spirit,
Great shining sloes with silver souls;
On the shore a priest was speaking
Of hermits and of peace and healing.

A Boy on his Bike

A boy upon a new bike of his own
That day as he cycled from home;
It might have been his own chariot
And he could have been a Ben Hur.

He was cycling out into the country
To go to see some ponies he loved;
He was happy to be out on his own,
Going down the road he knew well.

The ponies ran round the field freely,
Their manes flowing wild in the wind;
He who used to talk to them kindly
Too soon would be tragically killed.

His dead body was found by the sea,
Near the strand many long miles away,
Lying beneath the bushes and briars-
Last seen on a bike, back on that day.

The long days of searching were over,
The one that was lost was now found;
Their priest stood praying over him,
Quiet Gardaí, some crying, all round.

We all had been rocked to our roots
To hear a lad like him was laid low;
Many had come to help in the search-
He could have been one of their own.

So we'll remember him sadly forever
As he set out on the high road of life,
We will always see him just as he was,
That time, but a young boy on his bike.

Seats in the Sun

Through St. Mary's stained glass windows
The sun that's setting near Mount Brandon
Beams across the aisle, the sacred way;
A warm ray highlighting the varnished seats
Around where we are kneeling at the side:
The two of us by the Stations of the Cross.

Totus Tuus-Totally Yours

A prince of peace has sat in Peter's chair;
He came to make his home in Rome
From Poland-the holy Pope John Paul.
With his crosier in his hand he travelled
Near and far to preach the word of God;
He was the first to be a pilgrim Pope-
To wipe the world's tear stained face;
He kissed the ground we walked upon
And told all young people "I love you!"
The man who gave a lasting gift to us-
Of himself and told us to be always true:
Semper fidelis; vowing he was totus tuus.

Aux Anges

Une nuit du vent et de la pluie
Elle me vint en rêve sans bruit;
Une très belle hirondelle dans l'air,
Dans la tente au bord de la mer.

Je lui lentement étendis les bras,
Doucement elle descendit sur la main;
À mon coté mon amour apparut
Et avec plaisir je lui offris l'oiseau.

Elle tendrement accepta l'hirondelle-
Le symbol de l'amour éternal:
En rêvenant à nous tous les étés
En dépit de longs voyages de l'étranger.

Et puis elle me confessa gentiment
Qu'elle s'était senti très seul également,
En pensant à la nuit à la maison-
Les aux revoirs à l'idylle et sa saison.

Mais l'orage mit fin vite au bonheur
De retrouver l'amour de mon cœur;
Je me reveillai un être aux anges
En mélangent ces mots à sa louange.

OVER THE MOON

On a night of high wind and of rain
Into my dreaming it silently came
As I lay in my tent by the sea-
A most beautiful swallow to me.

I gladly warm welcomes extended
Then on my palm gently it landed;
The swallow I gave to my love
Who came to me soft as a dove.

The look on her face was so tender
At the sign of true love that I gave her:
To Ireland it comes back with loyalty
Despite the long flight and its frailty.

She spoke to me and shyly confided
That my loneliness was not one sided,
That often she thought of the evening,
The goodbyes to romance at leaving.

Then the scene in the dream it ended-
By a storm it was sadly suspended;
Awaking, her praises I put to a tune,
Floating about- I was over the moon.

RED DEER

Red deer at dawn that come our way,
Quick and sleek and nimble, nibbling;
Drifting fog is weaving morning magic
Beyond the ruined castle by the lake.

Sensing there is someone somewhere,
On red alert their heads are raised;
Silently they fade away like daybreak,
Disappearing through the lakeside reeds.

An Eye on London

The morning sky has a crest of a moon
Sitting up over my window's horizon.
Tall conifers compete with chimney stacks,
Castle top turrets and white office blocks;
The trickling traffic from King's Cross below
Meets life coming into the city.

It's quiet out there at four in the morning,
(The calm before the storm),
While the lights of the street lamps
Grow dimmer towards dawn
From my fourth floor eye on old London.

BEFORE THE BOMBING

Crossing elegant Victoria railway station
She reaches for her ringing mobile phone:
Young and yet without an ounce of fear,
Still moving onward as it sings its signal.
She answers, smiling with sincere delight-
And who is to tell it's not her father calling
Just to say hello and ask if she's alright.

A strict security warning mars the morning,
Insinuating the existence of an evil enemy
Who indiscriminately maim and cruelly kill,
Like the madmen did in the city of Madrid.

BLEEDING

Sliabh Aughty, my own mountain mine,
Rhododendroned ridge ever there for me;
Fields ascending higher as I go
From Ballylee to Loughrea's lake:
To look beyond at County Clare
Or to gaze at Galway Bay.

Beyond the vision of the valley
Is a village hard to find,
But now it's known the world over
Since the bog has moved in Derrybrien.

Forests, farms, furze and heather-
Colour palette in the sun:
Who'll protect them from the landslide
Slipping down the river run?

Noble men of Tobar Pheadair,
Castleboy and old Kilchreest
Won't you worry for your brothers
Who are threatened by the beast
Now let loose on this landscape
Far beyond the mountain top?
Have you seen Abhainn dá Loilioch?
Floating Christmas trees and peat
Slowly slithering towards Lough Cutra,
Killing brown trout in the squeeze,
Ruining roadways and the bridge.

Up in the pub that's warm and snug
There's talk and tension in the air:
They're telling tales of a fearsome gorge-
Up a thousand feet from there.

All the experts are left thinking
For they've failed to fight the flow:
All their barriers were upended
With a muffled mountain roar.

In Derrybrien they're not fearing
What's gone down but what's to come -
Maybe further bigger landslides!
For God's sake what's to be done?

Bring them help,
We fought for freedom-
'Tis their land, their place, their lives!
It's not just a piece of mountain -
Don't be fooled, it's far more grand;
Those who are up there isolated
Are the very salt of our native land.

When Pádraig Pearse was writing poetry
'Twas not of Golden Vales he wrote
But of the little towns of Connacht,
Of mountain fields that men have sown.

At the weekend Fleadh of Cooley-Collins
I watched a lively woman dance
In sean nós style and quiet abandon
On an afternoon in Peterswell;
While at the bar there played a fiddler,
With hat of tweed and stoic face,
His bowing was so soft and gentle
In deep respect to this great place.

Just one word about the mountain
That I grew beside secure,
Thinking mountains were forever-
They were there aloft alone;
But having been to Costa Blanca,
In a town called Guardamar,
There I saw the bulls tormented
In the ring to loud acclaim;
Such noble, haughty, well built creatures
Sent to death by lance and spear;
There they lost their way so blindly
And the blood flowed down their shanks.
Now it's nature's turn to suffer
As the bog slides o'er its floor-
Like the toros proud it's blameless,
All the shame is ours alone.

Let Spanish bulls on prados prance,
Far away from the mob's olés,
To be there to see in all their beauty
Like the backdrop of these hills.

'Twas not a bull but the Celtic Tiger
Changed your serene mountain stance:
What you'll see is masts and turbines
Every time you upwards glance.

Throw up your head and horns on high,
You wild and fearsome toro,
While the river of mud, the mountain's blood,
Flows from the land of Lough Atorick.

BONO AND BOB

Bono and Bob in Live Eight in Hyde Park:
Our boys are doing the business;
Heroes of rock and heralds of hope
Across the broad bands of the media.

African famine could soon be just history
For the Global Eight are dropping their debt
In the hope of an end to all the corruption.

In the far fields of Africa drums will beat
At the news from our Bob and our Bono;
They'll walk with a happier step in the heat
While their war is won simply with music.

CANNED

You can-
I'll be damned
But
Tonight
I need
To hold
One of you
In my hand.

You can-
You are
My only man.

You can-
You won't
And I can't
Be on our own.
I'll have another
And you there
Don't tell
My mother!

You can-
Now I can't
Stand.
Too many
Cans-
Going to land!
My fellowman
I'm canned.

I'll soon be
Ignominiously
Banned.

DEADLINES

The piano man plays on
And the tenors thrill
On the screen this Christmas;
Soon at dawn, it's said,
Saddam Hussein will hang.
Is that the only strategic plan?
Will the Sunnis and the Shiites
Still kill each other if they can?
Because he laid waste to those
Who did not tow the party line
He dies. Another death-
And did he have those weapons
Of destruction after all?

All was bad in the city of Baghdad
Before Saddam went on the run.
That it's bad again today
Is getting easier to say
As peoples lives are blown away
By waves of suicide bombers.

Washed up like flotsam
In our face from faraway
To reach our TV screens:
Dead bodies making news
For deadlines,
As regular as the tidal flow.

Fifteen more are dead;
How many more to go?
The piano plays on regardless
And the tenors raise the roof
But around that deadly gallows
In the capital of war
The only one with dignity
Is the man condemned to die-
And the hangman deals the cards.

IMAGINE IF

Oh God above forgive me
In the middle of this night;
Yet by the power of Heaven
The universe is all but mine.

I hear the silence and it means
I'm on my own. I'm here.

The mirror of this moment's real.
What I see I also deeply feel:
The shape and size of my own cell.

The door's the first I see so well:
It's in my eyes, it's always closed;
It's never mine the space it's in-
The prison owns that piece of light
And stores it up far out of sight.
It's not for me but my day will come
I'll stand there free like everyone
To take the road that starts off there;
So maybe now I'll say a prayer.

Thank God I have this time to think
Of how I stepped back from the brink.
I'm still your friend-I hope so God.
The walls say yes to me aloud.

My bed is there behind me flat:
Dreams come seldom where I'm at.

Not too far off another day
Will slowly push the heavy stone away
That makes this place so like a tomb
And I will travel towards the light;
I'll leave this room, I'll leave this womb,
I'm on my painful journey down.
It's awful dark. I'm on my own.

Now black is not that black at all-
If it fades much more I'm going to fall!

Little light of day, my eyes are open.
I'm glad my God that you have spoken:
Now I am yours and you are mine-
Daylight at last and still there's time.

THE SILENCER

I travelled on the Luas at last:
A silent maiden voyage
Across Seán Heuston Bridge,
Its brazen tracks had taken.

By red bricked ill gotten streets,
Deserted faded and neglected.

Only a single one-way traffic lane
The silent snake has left beside it
As it steals through Jervis Street
And by The Smithfield Market
To the very heart of Dublin city-
Still without a sound-the silencer.

BY THE POND

Kookaburras came like Carmelites
Arriving reverently in twos;
Landing quietly without a coo
On the paperbark tea trees
By the pond.

The silence snaps suddenly
At the Kookaburra's laugh.

A ballet corps of blue water lilies
Ready to dance.

MONTMARTRE

By metro to the ancient Montmartre hills
Where windmills once steadily turned
To mill the grain and to crush the grape;
Artists who adorn this place with art
Will paint you there in La Place du Tertre.

Inside the dimly lit Salle de Saint Pierre
I saw an enthralling expo of ancient dolls:
Elegant ones made in La Belle Epoque
Then some primitive poupées from Peru;
Pins in old African ones to work voodoo.

The snow melts slow and so silently falls
Off a tree that's high in the sloping green
And I take one more cup of café au lait-
Drinking to the pearl of Paris out there,
The jewel on the crown-the Sacre Coeur;
Three rising, winding Byzantine domes
All in white, this grand landmark in stone:
Basilica of all travellers and pilgrims true,
Capped by The Cross up high in the blue.

Another day over, the cafés are closing:
Candles on tables for two are blown out—
The secrets of love on faces were seen;
Banter of people now out on the streets—
Glowing from wine and of being together:
So happy and merry in twos and in fours,
Fixing of scarves and tumbling out doors.

EARLY TRAIN

Emerging from the station dimly lit,
The Dublin train confronts the dark;
Cruising comfortably out of Kerry
Before careering headlong onwards
Across the county bounds with Cork.

Then the dawn of everlasting beauty
Waves high her magic wand of light,
Revealing lines of long sensuous hills:
Their dips and curves mysterious,
Black against a deep blue low horizon.

Millstreet silhouetted there beyond,
Still lit up as if by Chinese lanterns.

 Banteer bathed in the morning glory-
The far off windows splashed with gold;
Tea is served, the next stop is called,
Awaking sleeping early morning risers.

HEAD OF THE CLAN

About you Mike I could write a book
If I was worthy to put you into words;
Yourself could put it better I believe.
Death has left us at a loss without you.

Going to fairs with seasoned farmers,
To them you were the old lad's son,
But fully fledged you surprised them:
Dealers now bargained with a man.

You arrived on call when skill was all,
Weather fair or foul the job was done
And you freely gave of what you got-
A farmer who had loyalty to the land.

As time went on they'd take their turn,
Hardworking men came hurrying in
To meadows when the hay was down
Or cattle testing time had come again.

Agile, red haired, in faded blue shirt:
Reins a bandoleer for him in spring
Guiding plough horses by the furrow,
Seagulls following–a storm warning.

Sheep shearing time, greasy fleeces,
Bottled stout for neighbours helping;
Sharing, swearing, telling good ones,
Among friends feeling free and easy.

On a kitchen chair he'd kneel to pray
In the morning as in the old tradition;
After he'd herd the sheep and cattle
And then he tilled in fields till evening.

By night after earning his daily bread
He felt the need of some good libation
And on his high stool he so often said
'I'm luckier than most'- in celebration.

Head of the clan, how I miss that man.
We had our nights in Lisdoonvarna;
Saved turf together on the mountain,
Mended the fence down by the river.

I write these lines for an absent brother
Buried on a hill up in Kilchreest village;
From here or from heaven overlooking
Forever the beloved land of our fathers.

LATE NIGHT TAXI

In the still night
I surface
From the dreamy depths;
There is a diesel drone
That plays upon my brain:
A taxi from the town
Bringing home
A small-time punter,
Elegant even at this hour;
Punch drunk from winning
At the races today.

In town tonight
Winners and losers were alright.

Heels in the hall,
A sound so safe:
A welcome noise in the night.
As she beelines to her bed
Her taxi turns and fades away.

MORNING STAR

Like a barnacle glued to a rock
She slept in her bed unrelenting,
Unconscious of each early call
After a weekend of merriment.
We drove for the train in Tralee-
Already the engine was throbbing;
A puff and hot tea on the platform
Before boarding to go to Cork city.

Going home on the road to Listowel,
The lights of North Kerry below me
Gave way to brilliance of blue
That grew in the heavens above.
The eastern colours were spreading
Over the back of Stack's mountains;
I could see silhouettes of the trees,
The morning star shining so brightly.

PUMPKIN SOUP

Seagulls standing in a windswept field
Look exactly like the way I feel
After leaving London on a Sunday afternoon.
Slowly mile by mile the night comes down
With a kind of November melancholy.
On either side we see the country wide
Where the trees still wear their leaves
And sheep their pastures graze on hillsides
Overlooking sweeping fields, some ploughed,
Some showing winter corn freshly sown.

Stansted airport draws near; dear daughter,
The joy of being with you still echoes in us
As we eat the fudge you gave us in Victoria.
Meanwhile you are making pumpkin soup-
At least that's what you said you'd do
On getting back to Crofton Road in Camberwell.

BADGERS IN THE WOOD

Stopped in our tracks
We stood in the wood
Seeing her pass before us:
She was the badger black and grey
Who shared our sylvan glenside.

Barely breathing in wonderment,
We watched the quiet manoeuvre
As her three cubs in single file
Followed closely behind their mother.

They all had their birth
In their sett in the earth
Beneath an old ash on the hillside.

Today their thirst made them bold
To take their pathway of old
Down to the pool in the stream
To have a long drink of cool water.

They are known to be shy
Of the sun when it's high,
To hunt by the moon till daybreak.

We have new life in our glen
And imagine the thrill
To meet in our blue belled woodland.

CAT ON THE STREET

She closes the door as she steps outside
At the end of her day's designing;
Stooping she greets a cat on the street
Whose bushy tail it exceeds him.
He's thrilled he is at this midnight hour
To meet with a lady of fashion.

While head to head they talk and purr,
Her handbag slung low from her shoulder,
He takes good note of its soft leather look
Like the feel of her hands that caressed him.

He swishes his tail on his way up the town,
Slipping in through the dimly lit archway;
At the end of the day he was only a stray
And he was after being treated like gentry.

FALL OF THE FLEDGLING

In the grass beneath the noisy rookery
The frightened fledgling crow I found:
He lay there flattened and diminished
By his fall from grace from far above.
I said I'd try to change his awful luck.

Raucous caws from a beak from *Jaws,*
When hungry, would go strangely silent
After he had swallowed what I fed him.
Satisfied, the little orphan went to sleep-
My mystery guest of feathered blackness.

He was not well this morning: sad to say
He died. I had my hopes that he'd survive
(I felt sad that I would never see him fly);
As he left, the light he lit was turned out.
I can only try to understand the darkness.

Like an Alien

That Sunday afternoon,
Out on the verdant lawn
On the verge of the wood
An alien stood:
Well it could have been!

I came back to earth
And looked again:
It was a Sika stag-
Head on;
Straight-up antlers-
Antenna like.
No more doubt;
Strangers staring: daring.
Still no move.

Head down, grazing:
This noble animal icon
An honour to behold-
Past glories of centuries
Only a look away.

Out of bounds here,
Far from the herd
And mountain forests,
Making me a part of time,
Sharing his wild life-
Until the sounds of children
Made him swing about,
His tail a flash of white.

Back to the wood he fled
As if he never was-
My strong brown Sika deer.
Now I often look and think
That he might reappear.

Rustic Fellow

A fox cub calmly crossed before me
And I brought my motor to a stop,
To respect a fox's daily right of way-
Bulldozed one day against his will.

Pulling in from the flow I saw him go.
He was naive and young and shy;
Stopping in his tracks, head high,
He stood there asking why of me.

He gave me a lingering look of blame
All the way over as far as his cover;
We had invaded the private space
Of a wild and worthy rustic fellow.

BAREFOOT

Scents of the summer incense to his senses,
The boy walks barefoot most of the way.
By hills of furze bushes above the soft bog,
Though ever so slowly, the river flows free
Through flower beds of bright yellow wild iris
Where the black water hens hide every day.

In meadows the cowslips all are in bloom
But he has to hurry on fast to his school;
Beneath his bare feet he feels the wet dew.
As the startled hare springs out of his lair
He leaves in his wake a wash of light spray-
His four paws are flying, ears up, he's away.

SNAKES ALIVE

Watched the African snake handlers
As they drew their bread and butter
Unceremoniously out of canvas sacks
And dared us, standing there in awe
Of writhing bodies and darting fangs,
To coil them round our necks for fun.
Some of us buried our fears to dare;
Afterwards to be no worse for wear:
Their masters from Morocco gripped
The snakes behind each moving head
To let them free meant we were dead.

Coming from the Casbah

And then we left the Casbah in Morocco,
Coming down a long and winding stairs,
And upwards came an entourage at speed
With a sheep for sacrifice, a helter skelter,
In celebration of the feast of Eid Al Adha,
Allah's sparing of the son of Abraham,
At the end of their Ramadan, family time;
Tangier youths unstoppable in their stride.
We stepped aside and then in my inner eye
I could have been away on Calvary's hill
As the Holy Lamb of God was passing by.

CÚCHULAINN'S SONS

In the annals of Cúchulainn's sons
Appear the names of our ancestors;
Time of Land League, landlords and evictions
When our Gaelic Games were spawned
While we waited for the dawn of freedom;
Floating on a tide of national pride
From the nineteenth to the twentieth century.
Barefoot players on pitches improvised,
Tournaments and marching bands
Of brass and reed and fife and drum:
The baronies hurling the troubled years away
With camáns shaped like camógs;
The flying sliotar a harbinger of peace
Sending shivers down the spine of time,
Raising up our ancient race
To feel again our rightful nationhood.
Running on—this fever in the blood,
Leaving to posterity dexterity and style-
Present on the field of play today
In the genes of great grand children,
Accurate as them in every game
In their aim from centre field or side line cut
And we cheer them from the stands
For they are Cúchulainn's youngest sons.

Exit 9

Shannon Airport is at Exit 9—
That way went each of mine;
An embrace to say goodbye:
Time enough the time to cry.
Last looks at departure gate—
Another wave but it's too late.
Words we had meant to say
Now must wait another day;
Like two bare trees we stand—
Isolated in departure land.

FROM THE PROM

Uplifted sunglasses on women who small chat
Over coffee at the terrazzo tables in Torrevieja;
The pretty coloured one is oh so chicly shaded,
Facing the February sun, dipping at five o'clock.

Meanwhile I'm playing musical chairs in vain
To escape the glare; green palm trees grouped
Over my head, my only allies now above me;
Beneath the tables there are sparrows hunting.

Like the anchored ship that now is setting sail
Tomorrow we'll go back to bitter wintry winds
Where the swallows nests are empty under eaves;
Today I saw them fly over our apartment *attico*.

Raiding ocean waves erode the red volcanic rock
But on the beach the water laps and plays around
In semi circles; sometimes crashing suddenly,
Causing me to awake from hypnotic sea sonatas.

The strolling couples take pictures from the prom
Of castles and cathedrals not built of solid stone
By architects or builders but by a busker bold-
A new Gaudi with the shifting sands of centuries.

NEW ROADS

On the western brim of Leith Hill,
Looking at all of North of Kerry,
There was a long blind bend
In the shape of a semicircle.

Now that has been cut off
To be replaced forever
By a new road climbing over-
Cut into the hill like the bed of a river.

I'll miss that scenic semicircle:
Perfumed primroses in the sun
Displayed along the grassy ditch,
Dressed in yellow every one.

Only a brief look at the seaside
From the wheel as you drove by:
To the west a long low valley
That stretched to Ballyheigue;
For it was a risky business
To be flirting with the view,
Not knowing what's behind you-
Maybe a big black four by four!
The boot is down, the window up,
This time you'd see no more.

I have waited for the moment
The new road straight and wide
Would surmount this hill in Kerry
And we'd have take off to the sky;
To be on the latest low horizon
Above Tralee the town deep down
And sleeping sleek Sliabh Mish
Of fleeting shadows one by one;
Of a tragic but romantic tale
Of a lovely rose born in the vale
And of her exiled lover and his lament
When the fair one died for love of him.

In its ballrooms of blushing roses
I sowed the wild oats of my life;
My Ford Cortina that I loved
Could almost drive home by itself-
Each hill and dale we knew so well.

The contours of Stack's Mountains
Have been embedded in my brain:
I see them when I'm driving
Through the wide and fertile plains
But I think that it's a holy shame
That they are acupunctured
By those wind turbines-such a sight!
White phantoms of the future?
Not at a price this high let there be light.

This is it at last—a sight to be seen!
This stretch of rising road, this dream:
From the blueprint to the masterpiece
Of many giant machines and men;
After all the excavation of the earth
It was filled with stone and chips,
Then the rolling and the tarring hot
And the building of its rising hips-
Each sloping down, green grassed,
Replacing what was taken at the start.

But I won't forget the bend beyond.
I will slip off this road some day
To see if there are still primroses,
To view the bright and distant bay.
Now I'll make a wish and welcome
A smooth black shining motorway.

SUNDAY SHOES

On Sundays for mass he would wear his good shoes:
To be ready they were always polished on Saturdays;
With pride in each stride he went around by the road.
The shortcut he took to his school Monday morning.

Scenting another hot summer climbing over the walls,
In bare feet through the fields he made his way freely
He skirted flotillas of furze in yellow blossoms ablaze;
On its bank he followed the flow of the lazy bog river.

Through beds of wild iris small black water hens play-
He would love to stay for the day to better his learning;
In lush meadows the cowslips and buttercups bloomed
Though he kept to the path and didn't pick any of them.

The strong startled hare shot straight up from his lair,
Ears up he took off in the bright dew of the morning;
His race was for freedom, his peace was disturbed,
Now he lightly springs up on a stonewall of limestone;

Looking back in distain at this lad so docile and tame,
He was away on his own out of view and free and easy;
Crossing over the bridge the boy put on his old shoes
To walk on the tar road down to the old schoolhouse.

CORNFIELDS

This year's maize turns green to yellow,
Ripening by the hour in Healy's fields:
Corn with a continental look,
Growing near the grotto in Killocrim;
Showing off its kilt of summer sheen
To your left and to your right;
Waving acres reaching to the river Feale
Where philosophical fishermen unwind.

EMBRACE

Bedecked with fans of ferns and little purple flowers,
Glad earth if you but could raise your lips to mine
And someway sling your leafy arms around my neck
I would lay with you and forever be your nature lover.

On the road that tops the hill and leads to Coolnaleen
We scent the summer hedgerows in the heat of day,
Remarking all the milestones like a low strong oak
Or gentle smooth young beeches and the wily ash.

Yellow furze and flagger by a hidden stream below;
Dashes of red roses and little strawberries ripening-
From the gateways fields are shaven from the baling,
Charolais as well within and the mountains far away.

HERON

Grey heron on black water,
Standing deadly still on stones;
In midstream a river shadow.

Ceist agam Orm

Ceist agam orm féin:
Ó chrann atá lom
Cad é an síor gearán
Sa choill atá láimh liom?
An éan atá ann?

Ní fheicim aon éan-
Níl éan ar an gcrann.

Cuirim cluas orm fein,
Ag féachaint in airde,
Is aithním an fhuaim uaim
Ar deireadh mar ghíoscán:
Fuinseoig ag caoineadh,
Ina luascán ag gaotha,
Ag fulaingt mar dhuine.

I Ask Myself

What's that?
That sound from the wood!
Does that bare tree complain a lot?
It does not!
It cannot be.
Is it the call of a bird?
It might maybe.

But high on its boughs
I can't see a thing:
Not a sign I see.

I listen in, all ears,
And found out now
That the sound
That had puzzled me
Came after all
From the tall old ash tree,
Creaking in pain,
In vain to complain
Of the way that the wind
Blows to bow and to bend it.

A reminder to me
That the suffering of man
Sounds so much the same
In everything but name.

Lambs

By the last rays of the winter sun
I seem to smell the signs of spring.
Those ewes we'd bring
Into the shelter of this lofty barn,
Its back turned against the gales,
Clean straw beds among the bales.

Young lambs learn quick to stand,
To find the ewes that fuss around
And knock them off to stand again
On spindly legs like drunken men.
I remember all these happy things
And later saw them dance in rings.

LAND OF THE LEACHTÁNS

The slow call of a crow outside
Seems to echo back to childhood-
To a sloping sunburnt hill
In the land of limestone leachtáns
And grey stone walls I'll always love;
Where we saved the hay together,
Often watching out for rain
And hurrying if we felt a drop or two-
Resting only when my mother came
With tea and rhubarb tart at four o'clock.

My father smoked his pipe contentedly,
Blessed himself and spat on his palms;
Resuming play we both made hay
And trimmed and tied each work of art.

With the brown pony we all called Dan,
My brother Mike, sunburned and strong,
Gathering in the hay with a tumble rake.

A curlew calls mysteriously-
Drawing back the veil of night,
Reminding me of Bailemhóinín
And the Carheen river quietly flowing
From Lios an Fhíona,
Draining the low black bogland,
Scenting sweet with furze and heather.

Landing Place

I can see afar those flowing fields
Sloping down from old stone walls
To that deep and embedded dip-
Cupping the presence of the pond
For thirsty cows and cattle around.

Rush and reed hide water hens;
Landing place for goose and duck,
And its swans unexpectedly return
In peace as straying memories do.

Spell bound pond in Tír na nÓg,
Treasury of young dreams of love;
Frost its face had frozen over-
Our sliding place in the setting sun.

TAILBACK

In a traffic jam and I can see
Daffodils bedeck the ditches,
Benches in a people's park.

Sideways there is a swamp
Where in the water preening
Stands a swan unperturbed.

A proud heron flies up above:
Once a tall and lordly one
Upheld its native landing rights,
Strutting around the grass
Within a nearby roundabout,
Reclaiming its own wetland.

As my patience in the tailback
Further ticks away from me
A brazen ambulance overtakes
This queue of cars and breaks
With flashing lights of blue
The traffic rules to save a life
By Limerick's Shannonside
Across The Whistling Bridge.

Meeting Wordsworth

I'd reached a clearing in the wood
And there I think I met Wordsworth:
As happy as he was by 'sylvan Wye'
When first I lived within his poems
And often walked with him in step.
The poet who told us in his lines
Of his God in nature, written above
His 'Tintern Abbey'I read and loved
And visited in later life in sunshine:
A ruins to remember for its peace.

WILD STRAWBERRIES

Rustling the ditch's floral skirt for strawberries:
Red and wild, elusive little rubies of delight,
Hidden as they hang, no bigger than a haw-
Vying with the velvet bells of purple foxgloves,
Filling the colour void and ringing out the days
Of violets fading in the shady wood unseen;
Overlooked by ferns in unfurled flags of green.

Aux Pied de La Croix

Du balcon de ma chambre en haut,
Un matin à Medugorje d'or doux
La vallée s'est baignée au soleil levant,
Les coqs des villages ensemble exultants.
Dehors au coin du petit potager la bas
La fumée monte d'un feu aux cieux,
Mais qu'est-ce qu'ils font si tôt avec
Les tuyaus dans le tonneau d'eau?
On dit ici qu'il y a des petites distilleries
Qu'ils font du Schnapps, bonne à boire:
Ces gens choisis de nôtre Mère
Dans ce lieu bénit entre ciel et terre.
Vicka la visionnaire de la Vierge Marie,
De la voix débordée de la joie d'esprit;
Pendant qu' elle nous de l'abri parlait
La pluie en Bosnie sur la foule tombait.
Jacov modestement de ses visions parlait:
"Il n'y a aucun artiste pour décrire sa beauté;
Les beaux yeux sont bénis d'amour infini
Et sa voix maternelle est une vraie mélodie."
Les jeunes toxicomanes en santé libérés
Guidaient les pèlerins au Dome foulé-
C'est l'heure de l'apparition pour Mirjana,
Sa réunion sacrée avec la Reine de la Paix.
Le démon qui criait dans le corps d'une fille,
Vert de peur de la présence de Marie,
Il se tu d'aboyer quand Elle pris la parole;

Le soleil a dansé—un disque bleu doré.
Dieu et son peuple à Podbrodo en harmonie;
Les pèlerins se rassemblent au pied de la Croix.
Descendant enjoué à la messe matinale
Les cloches au loin sonnent très musicales.
Le parfum de roses-de Sa présence si douce
Senti au chapelet à St. Jacques le soir;
Le choeur chante en croate un fervent cantique,
A l'ouest au soleil—une manifestation mystique.
Ecouter les grillons et les chiens de ce quartier,
Regarder la lune, la gardienne de la nuit;
Si le monde un jour change et choisit la paix
Bien sûr on commence à Medugorje.

MEDUGORJE

I breathe from my upstairs bedroom balcony
The air of a soft golden morning in symphony:
The crowing of cocks for Medugorje's new dawn,
In the valley so silent in the heat of the sun.
Outside in the garden, in the corner there,
Smoke from a fire incensing the air;
Those men walking around and I wonder why
There's pipes from the barrel that's standing close by.
Some speak of mini distilleries here,
Of spirits called Schnapps, your life to cheer,
And the chosen people of the Virgin Mother
In the days of war lived in peace with each other.
Vicka the visionary of the Holy Queen,
Whose joy was truly a sight to be seen,
Stood by her door her story to tell
As the rain on our Bosnian brollies fell.
Jacov spoke of Her beauty so quietly:
"To be able to paint Her was highly unlikely;
Her heavenly eyes are best described blest;
Her voice is a melody," with love he confessed.
Liberated young addicts of the Cenacolo Home
Directing us all who had come to their Dome;
They usher in Mirjana , very soon to be given
A message of peace from the Queen of Heaven.
Loud crying in fear from a girl possessed
At the coming of Mary, for the demon no rest.
His barking so evil stamped out by Her glory;

The gilded blue disc of the sun told the story.
God and his people on Podbrodo in harmony;
Around the White Cross the feeling was heavenly;
Descending fulfilled to the mass in the morning
The bells from afar were musically charming.
The stray scent of roses at the Rosary was stunning
In the Church of St. James at the time of Her coming ;
The Croatian hymns were fervent and constant
And the sun in the west was now a gold monstrance.
The crickets sing on between the hills stark
As the full moon is guarding the night from the dark;
If the world is to change and have peace in its heart
Medugorje is the place where we'll make a new start.

East to Latvia

They are a people quiet and deep,
The Latvians: here in Riga
They remember Ninety One-
The year the Russians left.

In the centre of Boulevard Brivibas
At the monument they call Milda
Two soldiers guard with honour
The freedom of a young Republic.

On the Duagava in a Bateau-Mouche
Upon its riverbanks I saw from me
This city noted for its noveau art:
Alberta Street was Eizenstein's idea.

The Reval Hotel top reveals
Weather cocks on timeworn churches;
The fine cathedral's five cupolas
Are gleaming gold as the sun sets.

Their Cardinal in his purple cap
On the altar steps for mid-day mass;
The silent Luthern pews for prayer,
Greek Orthodox weddings in pairs.

By our restaurant in Doma Square
Smoothly pass the Cadillac cars,
Bouncing along the cobblestones;
A happy girl goes home with flowers.

Hurling Hero

Maroon and white clad hurler,
Galway's hero so swift and strong;
'John Connolly is on'
They gladly shouted,
The long awaiting sideline throng;
From the dressing room he's running,
Pulling low and swinging high
In the hunt for Galway glory
On a summer's eve in Athenry.

Inferno

The wild creatures of the bog land
At midnight time of gentle sleep
All curled up in their slumbers
In furze bush and rush and reed
Had to flee in frightened flurry
From a sudden racing raging fire.

Each furze in turn first crackled
Then it blazed high into the sky,
Lifting off the cloak of darkness
Where I look down from the hill,
Overflowing shining light on me.

Our songbirds sleeping silenced
And the magic of that cuckoo's call
I heard I'll hear no more I fear.

Blue lights flash and sirens wail
On winding roads to this inferno.

Tonight our backroom bedroom
Is lit by burning bog land light
But tomorrow no furze in bloom
For me; only burnt black I'll see.

Sunday Morning

We thought the same on the shimmering sand,
By the towering cliffs with their tufts of green,
That here the time and the place was at hand
On a Sunday to savour the pleasure of being.

The passionate tide was out past the Point-
That Arc de Triomphe at the cliff's high head;
The playful waves our fears did anoint:
'To be or not to be' that's what Hamlet said.

Deep and black through the dark of the caves
Ran a ruthless river released by the sea,
Relentlessly entering the hall of Hades
Where no one would want ever to be.

So we looked aloft where the seagulls nest
In the cosy clefts high in rock above our heads;
In snow white pairs on their eggs they rest,
Screeching in bliss from their wedding beds.

Stack of shining rock red, black and brown,
With the water dripping from its sculpted face
To circles wheeling when we both look down
Into the pool of sunlit water at its sandy base.

Between ebb and flow our life time is short.
Neptune she rinses out all her seaweed hair
In the tide when it's high in this happy resort
And often the sea as it sighs falls asleep there.

Unknown

All on a day around they lay:
Unfinished poems in pieces;
Cups of tea about, half drunk,
Forgotten and turned cold.

As cold as poems unknown
Sent off to fight for life,
Often to die for dead poets
Who haunt themselves alone.

Vigil

The penny candle wick burned on still
In its shallow well of clear melted wax:
It was a prayer to seek Our Lady's care
In our bedroom on a night vigil in bed.
In Dublin's fair city, up in the Coombe,
Our daughter was soon to give birth.

Then all of a sudden our vigil was over
As the mobile beside me went wild
With the joyful news of a new baby girl!

Her dad's words at dawn so pulsating,
Like a shot of hot punch for the nerves;
With all the fresh pride of being a father
He talked of the baby's light brown hair
And the sound of her cry on being born.

Beside him her mother was feeding her,
Still tired from the labour of childbirth
But so happy to look down on the dream
That at break of day had been delivered.

Happy in our new life as grandparents
We drew the curtains to start a new day
As the light of the long burning candle
Went out just at the end of our prayers.

THE HAND OF MAN

It was the hand of Man not the will of God
Sealed their fate on their Haitian hillsides:
When the awful earth quake came to pass
The houses that were badly built collapsed;
Condemned for their impoverished lives,
Crying of sundered families suffering loss
Reaching many a mile to hardened hearts.
We now can compensate, albeit a little late,
For wilfully in our wealth forgetting Haiti.

DAYDREAM

When black clouds in the evening all hang low,
I can see no sunset and there is no afterglow,
My mind flies far until I land in sunny Thailand;
There for a change I am a turtle on the beach
That's snowy white beneath a canopy of blue.
Sliding down to sea and diving deep below
I swim above that rainbow coloured seabed,
Off the land of Thai: lost in the Isle of Koh Tao.

THE ROMANIAN

Seated at the entrance to an alley,
A music man on a shopping mall
Played his own plaintive melody
On a fine tuned Romanian fiddle
Attached to a shiny trumpet horn.
Playing to us, an elder of his race:
A conversation without speaking,
His heart and soul in his playing-
Saying what he couldn't say at all;
His brown felt hat upon his head,
His bike leant up against the wall.

In Transit

The sudden snow that fell last night
Now clothes a world struck silent
By snowflakes falling slowly
As magical as a million falling stars,
Softly settling down below on earth
A night as white as pale moonlight.
Into this Christmas card like scene
A Council friend came in the end
To grit the road with salt and sand
And twice he repelled the glassy ice
That had made my hill a skating rink.
I had to call my plumber in the thaw
Who with a spanner and a copper cap
Stopped leaking water from escaping
As easily as I would turn off a tap.
And all this while with a little smile
An optimistic exile prepared to go,
Her sights on sunrise in Vancouver;
Going from minus zero to minus zero,
In transit, our youngest hopeful hero.

Always Eighteen

The clearness of a dream
I had in bed last night
Has dimmed at dawn.
I'm awake, remembering,
Its dialogue in a deep sleep
Now almost vanished
In the wash of awakening.

In the dream, so real I swear,
She appeared:
Into my head as I slept she crept-
Always eighteen.
As lovely as I left her
At her father's hearth
As we said our last goodbyes
To all the years of my unspoken love.
'Love's Labour'- I began to say,
(Speaking of the title of a play)
But there she stopped me
In my mid line
To finish it herself this time:
'Love's Labour- is never- Lost'

Contradicting
Both Shakespeare and myself.
That was the only thing she said
As with the dream she left my bed.